THE
Word
BECAME
Flesh

THE

Word

BECAME

Flesh

Reflections for Advent and Christmas

Edited by Matthew Becklo

WORD
on FIRE.

Published by Word on Fire, Park Ridge, IL 60068
© 2022 by Word on Fire Catholic Ministries
Printed in the United States of America
All rights reserved

Cover design, typesetting, and interior art direction by Rozann Lee and Cassie Bielak

25 24 23 22   1 2 3 4

ISBN: 978-1-685780-21-0

Library of Congress Control Number: 2021922713

"The Word became flesh
and made his dwelling
among us."

—JOHN 1:14

Contents

Introduction

Friends, thank you for joining us at Word on Fire for this journey through the Advent and Christmas seasons.

Advent is the liturgical season of vigilance or, to put it more mundanely, of waiting. During the four weeks prior to Christmas, we light the candles of our Advent wreaths and put ourselves in the spiritual space of the Israelite people who, through many long centuries, waited for the coming of the Messiah: "How long, O LORD?" (Ps. 13:1).

Waiting is very hard for most of us. I suppose we human beings have always been in a hurry, but modern people especially seem to want what they want when they want it. We are driven, determined, goal-oriented, fast-moving. Waiting is especially hard when we see others experience, or experience ourselves, great struggles, anxieties, and sufferings. I am sure that every religious person, every believer in God, at some point wonders, "Why doesn't God just straighten everything out? Why doesn't the all-powerful and all-loving Creator of the universe simply deal with the injustice, suffering, violence, and sin that so bedevil his world?"

We can hear precisely this cry in the prophets of ancient Israel. All of them—Isaiah, Jeremiah, Ezekiel, Hosea, Zechariah, etc.—utter some version of "How long, O Lord?" One form that this expectation takes is a yearning that the God of Israel would come to reign as king—which is to say, as one who has the power and authority to right every wrong. A passage from the fifty-second chapter of the prophet Isaiah speaks exactly in these terms: "How beautiful upon the mountains are the feet of the one bringing good news, announcing peace, bearing good news, announcing salvation, saying to Zion, 'Your God is King!'" (Isa. 52:7). The prophet is envisioning the great day when Yahweh will take charge and set things right, when he will "bare his holy arm in the sight of all the nations" (Isa. 52:10)—that is to say, roll up his sleeve, asserting his dominance over his enemies.

The fundamental message of Christmas is that this prophecy has come true—but in the most unexpected way: "In the beginning was the Word, and the Word was with God, and the Word was God. . . . And the Word became flesh and made his dwelling among us" (John 1:1, 14). Jesus of Nazareth is not simply one more in a long line of prophets, not one more wisdom figure, not just another religious hero; rather, he is what Isaiah and his prophetic colleagues longed for: God himself in the flesh, come to rule. We know that kingly authority is involved in this enfleshment of God, for St. John reminds us: "What came to be through him was life, and this life was the light of the human race; the light shines in the darkness, and the darkness has not overcome it" (John 1:3–5). The evangelist is telling us that the Word has come to fight an enemy, and the enemy will not prevail.

I hope this booklet—which includes reflections, poems, and prayers from across two thousand years of Catholic history—draws you more deeply into the mysteries of the Advent and Christmas seasons: Israel's longing for the Messiah, the Annunciation to the Blessed Virgin by the angel Gabriel, the Incarnation of God in Mary's womb, the journey of Joseph and the Mother of God to Bethlehem, the Nativity of our Lord, and finally, the life of the Holy Family. In dwelling on these mysteries throughout this sacred time, may you come to a renewed encounter with the living reality of Christ, the "Wonderful Counselor, Mighty God, Everlasting Father, Prince of Peace" (Isa. 9:6).

Let us join the great men and women of our tradition, raising our eyes with vigilance for God's salvation—and receiving in our hearts the amazing grace of his Incarnation.

Peace,

+ Robert Barron

Bishop Robert Barron

The First
Week *of* Advent

THE MESSIAH

Scripture
Isaiah

7:14

Therefore the Lord himself will give you this sign:
    the virgin shall conceive, and bear a son,
    and shall name him Emmanuel.

9:1–6

The people who walked in darkness
    have seen a great light;
upon those who dwelt in the land of gloom
    a light has shone.
You have brought them abundant joy
    and great rejoicing,
as they rejoice before you as at the harvest,
    as people make merry when dividing spoils.
For the yoke that burdened them,
    the pole on their shoulder,
and the rod of their taskmaster
    you have smashed, as on the day of Midian.
For every boot that tramped in battle,
    every cloak rolled in blood,
    will be burned as fuel for flames.
For a child is born to us, a son is given us;
    upon his shoulder dominion rests.

They name him Wonder-Counselor, God-Hero,
  Father-Forever, Prince of Peace.
His dominion is vast
  and forever peaceful,
from David's throne, and over his kingdom,
  which he confirms and sustains
by judgment and justice,
  both now and forever.
The zeal of the LORD of hosts will do this!

11:1–10

On that day,
A shoot shall sprout from the stump of Jesse,
  and from his roots a bud shall blossom.
The spirit of the LORD shall rest upon him:
  a spirit of wisdom and of understanding,
  a spirit of counsel and of strength,
  a spirit of knowledge and of fear of the LORD,
  and his delight shall be the fear of the LORD.
Not by appearance shall he judge,
  nor by hearsay shall he decide,
But he shall judge the poor with justice,
  and decide aright for the land's afflicted.
He shall strike the ruthless with the rod of his mouth,
  and with the breath of his lips he shall slay the wicked.
Justice shall be the band around his waist,

and faithfulness a belt upon his hips.
Then the wolf shall be the guest of the lamb,
   and the leopard shall lie down with the kid;
The calf and the young lion shall browse together,
   with a little child to guide them.
The cow and the bear shall be neighbors,
   together their young shall rest;
   the lion shall eat hay like the ox.
The baby shall play by the cobra's den,
   and the child lay his hand on the adder's lair.
There shall be no harm or ruin on all my holy mountain;
   for the earth shall be filled with the knowledge of the
      LORD,
   as water covers the sea.
On that day, the root of Jesse,
   set up as a signal for the nations,
The Gentiles shall seek out,
   for his dwelling shall be glorious.

40:1–11

Comfort, give comfort to my people,
   says your God.
Speak tenderly to Jerusalem, and proclaim to her
   that her service is at an end,
   her guilt is expiated;

Indeed, she has received from the hand of the LORD
    double for all her sins.

    A voice cries out:
In the desert prepare the way of the LORD!
    Make straight in the wasteland a highway for our God!
Every valley shall be filled in,
    every mountain and hill shall be made low;
The rugged land shall be made a plain,
    the rough country, a broad valley.
Then the glory of the LORD shall be revealed,
    and all people shall see it together;
    for the mouth of the LORD has spoken.

A voice says, "Cry out!"
    I answer, "What shall I cry out?"
"All flesh is grass,
    and all their glory like the flower of the field.
The grass withers, the flower wilts,
    when the breath of the LORD blows upon it.
    So then, the people is the grass.
Though the grass withers and the flower wilts,
    the word of our God stands forever."

Go up onto a high mountain,
    Zion, herald of glad tidings;

Cry out at the top of your voice,
    Jerusalem, herald of good news!
Fear not to cry out
    and say to the cities of Judah:
    Here is your God!
Here comes with power
    the Lord God,
    who rules by his strong arm;
Here is his reward with him,
    his recompense before him.
Like a shepherd he feeds his flock;
    in his arms he gathers the lambs,
Carrying them in his bosom,
    and leading the ewes with care.

Reading
Bishop Barron
Article

We will never be adequately prepared for the coming of the Savior unless and until we feel in our bones that there is something we need to be saved from. If we don't require salvation, then Jesus devolves, very quickly, into one wise man among many, one more spiritual teacher in a long line of similar figures across space and time. The great and ancient Advent chant "O come, O come, Emmanuel, / And ransom captive Israel, / That mourns in lonely exile here / Until the Son of God appear" catches this fundamental Christian truth. Until we feel like prisoners held for ransom, men and women condemned to hopeless exile, we will not sing those words with anything even approaching conviction.

A passage from the sixty-third chapter of the prophet Isaiah provides a series of images that help us to articulate this sense of being in desperate need of salvation. "Why," Isaiah laments, "do you let us wander, O Lord, from your ways?" (Isa. 63:17). The trope of the path is a common one in the Scriptures: there is a way that we are meant to walk in the spiritual order, and the vast majority of us tend to lose it.

There is a feeling that now only people of a certain age remember, and that is the sensation of being well and truly lost. I limit this to older folks because today's hyper-sophisticated GPS tools usually permit us to find our destinations with ease. But prior to those wonderful gadgets, when we relied on maps or, more frequently, on directions scribbled on a piece of paper, we much more readily got lost. When I was about seventeen and hence a very inexperienced driver, I was making my way through the streets of Chicago, looking for an expressway entrance. I managed to miss it, and in short order, as darkness was coming on, I realized, with a uniquely sinking sensation, that I didn't really know where I was or where I was going.

Dante's *Divine Comedy* commences with these lines: "Midway on the journey of our life / I woke to find myself alone and lost in a dark wood / having wandered from the straight path." Even if you have found great success in your profession, and even if you are relatively satisfied in your relationships and your social standing, I would be willing to bet that, at the deepest level, you feel lost, and you don't really know where you are going. As Dante intuited, this insight often occurs when we are at midlife, but we all know the truth of it to varying degrees. As painful as it might be, move, this Advent, into that spiritual space. Feel what it's like to be off the path, disoriented. Then you will be able to cry out for the one who said, "I am the way, and the truth, and the life" (John 14:6).

A second lament from the prophet Isaiah is this: "Why do you . . . harden our hearts so that we fear you not?" For the biblical authors, the heart is the seat of emotion, thought, and action—the core of the personality. It is meant to be "soft" so that God might easily shape it according to his purpose. The hardened heart is like brittle, dry clay, which cracks and shatters at the merest touch of the divine potter. When we are obsessed with our own plans and projects, when we are preoccupied with the prerogatives of the ego, our hearts are hard. In his Letter to the Galatians, St. Paul utters this ecstatic cry: "It is no longer I who live but Christ who lives in me" (Gal. 2:20). This is the language of someone who has allowed his soft heart to be molded utterly by the Lord, who has exchanged the ego-drama for the theo-drama. During Advent, we should inquire after the quality of our heart. How have we been resisting the manner in which God wants to shape us? Only those who know that they are hard-hearted truly long for the arrival of the Sacred Heart.

A third and final Isaian complaint is this: "Behold, you are angry, and we are sinful; all of us have become like unclean people" (Isa. 64:4–5). It is difficult to read any two pages of the Bible in succession, Old Testament or New, and not encounter a reference to the divine anger. It will simply not do to set this idea aside, as though it were an unfortunate holdover from a benighted time. But we must be careful not to emotionalize the reference so as to suggest that God flies, like a raging, dysfunctional father, into a fit of pique. I would suggest that the divine anger is a beautifully apt metaphor for God's passion to set things right. When sin and injustice deface the beauty of God's beloved creatures and produce deep unhappiness in them, God cannot hold himself in. He rages, as it were, to rectify the situation.

Therefore, this Advent, we all ought to identify those actions and attitudes in us that rouse God's anger. I fully realize that the culture instructs us in a thousand ways to affirm our guiltlessness: "I'm okay, you're okay." But the Bible instructs us to admit to our "uncleanness." Once again, this is not an exercise in psychologically debilitating self-reproach; it is a courageous willingness to offer our weakness to the divine physician. It is allowing the God of justice to set things right in us. Until we do this, we will never appreciate the one who said, "I have come to light a fire on the earth" (Luke 12:49), and who, in magnificently high dudgeon, turned over the tables in the temple.

So lest Christmas become one more blandly secular holiday, let us all do some real Advent work: come to grips with how lost we are, how hardened our hearts have become, how we have stirred up God's anger.

Reflection
Fulton J. Sheen
Life of Christ

Socrates had no one to foretell his birth. Buddha had no one to pre-announce him and his message or tell the day when he would sit under the tree. Confucius did not have the name of his mother and his birthplace recorded, nor were they given to men centuries before he arrived so that when he did come, men would know he was a messenger from God. But with Christ it was different. Because of the Old Testament prophecies, his coming was not unexpected. There were no predictions about Buddha, Confucius, Lao-tze, Mohammed, or anyone else; but there were predictions about Christ. Others just came and said, "Here I am, believe me." They were, therefore, only men among men and not the Divine in the human. Christ alone stepped out of that line saying, "Search the writings of the Jewish people and the related history of the Babylonians, Persians, Greeks, and Romans." (For the moment, pagan writings and even the Old Testament may be regarded only as historical documents, not as inspired works.)

It is true that the prophecies of the Old Testament can be best understood in the light of their fulfillment. The language of prophecy does not have the exactness of mathematics. Yet if one searches out the various Messianic currents in the Old Testament, and compares the resulting picture with the life and work of Christ, can one doubt that the ancient predictions point to Jesus and the kingdom which he established? God's promise to the patriarchs that through them all the nations of the earth would be blessed; the prediction that the tribe of Judah would be supreme among the other Hebrew tribes until the coming of him whom all nations would obey; the strange yet undeniable fact that in the Bible of the Alexandrian Jews, the Septuagint, one finds clearly predicted the *virgin* birth of the Messiah; the prophecy of Isaiah 53 about the patient sufferer, the Servant of the Lord, who will lay down his life as a guilt-offering for his people's offenses; the perspectives of the glorious, everlasting kingdom of the House of David—in whom but Christ have these prophecies found their fulfillment? From a historical point of view alone, here is uniqueness which sets Christ apart from all other founders of world religions. And once the fulfillment of these prophecies did historically take place in the person of Christ, not only did all prophecies cease in Israel, but there was discontinuance of sacrifices when the true Paschal Lamb was sacrificed.

Poem
Thomas Merton
"Advent"

Charm with your stainlessness these winter nights,
Skies, and be perfect!
Fly vivider in the fiery dark, you quiet meteors,
And disappear.
You moon, be slow to go down,
This is your full!

The four white roads make off in silence
Towards the four parts of the starry universe.
Time falls like manna at the corners of the wintry earth.
We have become more humble than the rocks,
More wakeful than the patient hills.

Charm with your stainlessness these nights in Advent,
    holy spheres,
While minds, as meek as beasts,
Stay close at home in the sweet hay;
And intellects are quieter than the flocks that feed by
    starlight.

Oh pour your darkness and your brightness over all our
    solemn valleys,
You skies: and travel like the gentle Virgin,
Toward the planets' stately setting,
Oh white full moon as quiet as Bethlehem!

Hymn

Veni, Veni, Emmanuel

Latin

Veni, veni, Emmanuel!
Captivum solve Israel!
Qui gemit in exilio,
Privatus Dei Filio,

REFRAIN:
Gaude! Gaude! Emmanuel,
Nascetur pro te, Israel.

Veni, O Sapientia,
Quae hic disponis omnia,
Veni, viam prudentiae
Ut doceas et gloriae.
(REFRAIN)

Veni, veni, Adonai,
Qui populo in Sinai
Legem dedisti vertice
In maiestate gloriae.
(REFRAIN)

English

O come, O come, Emmanuel,
And ransom captive Israel,
That mourns in lonely exile here
Until the Son of God appear.

Rejoice! Rejoice! Emmanuel
Shall come to thee, O Israel.

O come, thou wisdom, from on high,
And order all things far and nigh;
To us the path of knowledge show,
And teach us in her ways to go.
(REFRAIN)

O come, O come, thou Lord of might,
Who to thy tribes on Sinai's height
In ancient times did give the law,
In cloud, and majesty, and awe.
(REFRAIN)

Veni, O Iesse virgula,
Ex hostis tuos ungula,
De specu tuos tartari
Educ et antro barathri.
(REFRAIN)

Veni, Clavis Davidica,
Regna reclude coelica,
Fac iter Tutum superum,
Et claude vias inferum.
(REFRAIN)

Veni, veni, O Oriens,
Solare nos adveniens,
Noctis depelle nebulas,
Dirasque noctis tenebras.
(REFRAIN)

Veni, veni, Rex Gentium,
Veni, Redemptor omnium,
Ut salves tuos famulos
Peccati sibi conscios.
(REFRAIN)

O come, thou rod of Jesse's stem,
From ev'ry foe deliver them
That trust thy mighty power to save,
And give them vict'ry o'er the grave.
(REFRAIN)

O come, thou key of David, come,
And open wide our heav'nly home,
Make safe the way that leads on high,
That we no more have cause to sigh.
(REFRAIN)

O come, thou Dayspring from on high,
And cheer us by thy drawing nigh;
Disperse the gloomy clouds of night
And death's dark shadow put to flight.
(REFRAIN)

O come, Desire of nations, bind
In one the hearts of all mankind;
Bid every strife and quarrel cease;
And fill the world with heaven's peace.
(REFRAIN)

Reflection
Pope St. John Paul II
Homily

"*Shower, O heavens, from above*" (*Rorate caeli*).

Advent is expressed in this supplication taken from the book of the prophet Isaiah. "Shower, O heavens, from above, and let the skies rain down righteousness; . . . let the earth open, that salvation may sprout forth" (see Isa. 45:8).

These are words of the prophet Isaiah. He is referring to the situation of his homeland, and from his observation of the parched land that needs water to blossom, he draws the analogy that expresses his people's expectation: the expectation of the promised Messiah, the Savior of Israel. Isaiah knows that the fulfillment of the promise can only come "from above," *from God*, like the rain that falls from the clouds. At the same time, in a no less precise way, the prophet foretells that the Messiah, the Savior of the world, will be born *on earth, as the blessed fruit of the root of Jesse*, according to the Lord's promise. He will come among the Chosen People and will be the fulfillment of that great "advent" that is the Old Covenant. . . .

God speaks to his people: "Fear not, I will help you. . . . I will help you. . . . Your Redeemer is the Holy One of Israel" (Isa. 41:13–14). "When the poor and needy seek water, and there is none, and their tongue is parched with thirst, I, the

Lord, . . . will open rivers on the bare heights, and fountains in the midst of the valleys; I will make the wilderness a pool of water, and the dry land springs of water" (Isa. 41:17–18). Thanks to this providential irrigation, the desert will bloom and produce fruit in abundance.

This metaphor, eloquent for those who have visited the desert areas of Palestine, recalls another harvest, the *harvest of souls*. The awaited Messiah will change the destiny of the people of Israel and of humanity: he will be able to draw an abundant harvest of the redeemed from a sterile desert.

Prayer

St. John Henry Newman

Meditations and Devotions

O Adonai, O Ruler of Israel, you that guide Joseph like a flock, O Emmanuel, O Sapientia, I give myself to you. I trust you wholly. You are wiser than I—more loving to me than I myself. Deign to fulfill your high purposes in me whatever they be—work in and through me. I am born to serve you, to be yours, to be your instrument. Let me be your blind instrument. I ask not to see—I ask not to know—I ask simply to be used.

    Amen.

Poem

G.K. Chesterton
"A Child of the Snows"

There is heard a hymn when the panes are dim,
    And never before or again,
When the nights are strong with a darkness long,
    And the dark is alive with rain.

Never we know but in sleet and in snow,
    The place where the great fires are,
That the midst of the earth is a raging mirth
    And the heart of the earth a star.

And at night we win to the ancient inn
    Where the child in the frost is furled,
We follow the feet where all souls meet
    At the inn at the end of the world.

The gods lie dead where the leaves lie red,
    For the flame of the sun is flown,
The gods lie cold where the leaves lie gold,
    And a Child comes forth alone.

"When the gentle light of
the Advent candles begins to shine
in the dark days of December—
a mysterious light in a mysterious
darkness—it awakens in us the
consoling thought that divine light,
the Holy Spirit, has never ceased
to illumine the darkness
of the fallen world."

—EDITH STEIN
(ST. TERESA BENEDICTA OF THE CROSS)

The Second
Week *of* Advent

THE
ANNUNCIATION

Scripture
Luke 1:26–38

The angel Gabriel was sent from God to a town of Galilee called Nazareth, to a virgin betrothed to a man named Joseph, of the house of David, and the virgin's name was Mary. And coming to her, he said, "Hail, full of grace! The Lord is with you." But she was greatly troubled at what was said and pondered what sort of greeting this might be. Then the angel said to her, "Do not be afraid, Mary, for you have found favor with God. Behold, you will conceive in your womb and bear a son, and you shall name him Jesus. He will be great and will be called Son of the Most High, and the Lord God will give him the throne of David his father, and he will rule over the house of Jacob forever, and of his Kingdom there will be no end." But Mary said to the angel, "How can this be, since I have no relations with a man?" And the angel said to her in reply, "The Holy Spirit will come upon you, and the power of the Most High will overshadow you. Therefore the child to be born will be called holy, the Son of God. And behold, Elizabeth, your relative, has also conceived a son in her old age, and this is the sixth month for her who was called barren; for nothing will be impossible for God." Mary said, "Behold, I am the handmaid of the Lord. May it be done to me according to your word." Then the angel departed from her.

Reading
Bishop Barron
Light from Light

From the Greek *Christos,* the term Christ renders the Hebrew *Mashiach*, which means "the anointed one." Though priests and kings were anointed in the ancient Hebrew tradition, the term is used most often and with greatest resonance of David, the greatest of Israel's kings. We find in 1 Samuel the moving account of the young David being anointed by the prophet Samuel: "And the spirit of the Lord came mightily upon David" (1 Sam. 16:13). David does indeed become a priest, since he brings the ark of the covenant into his new capital Jerusalem, leading a dance while wearing the distinctive garment of a priest. He also commences the preparations for the building of the temple, which will be completed by Solomon his son. The point is that David sees the reestablishment of right praise as essential to the success of his kingdom: all the tribes of the Lord united around the worship of the one God.

And David is assuredly king, indeed the greatest of Israel's leaders. His triumph was to have held off the enemies of the nation and to have expanded its borders so as to establish a kind of empire. This was, in the estimation of the ancient teachers of Israel, the mission given originally to Adam. Our first parent was meant not to remain self-satisfied in Eden, but rather to expand the borders of that paradise outward. One of the effects of the original sin is precisely a suspension, or at least compromising, of that mission. The various kings of Israel, to varying degrees, took up the Adamic task, but none realized it as fully as David.

However, what becomes eminently clear in the biblical account of King David is that, though he was to be sure a morally and spiritually imposing figure, he did not utterly fulfill his destiny. His priesthood is undermined by his frequent moral failures, most notably in connection with Uriah and Bathsheba; and his kingship is undermined by the rebellion of his son Absalom and by David's own laziness and inattention. And therefore Israel began to dream of a perfect or definitive David who would deal finally with the enemies of the nations, who would gather the scattered tribes of Israel, and who would restore right praise to the nation, and through the nation, to the world. This is the *Mashiach* whose coming the prophets predict and whose reign the Psalms celebrate in anticipation.

There is probably no greater anticipation of the coming of the definitive David than in the words spoken by the prophet Nathan to David himself (2 Sam. 7:12–17). The Lord has promised, the prophet tells the king, that the Lord will put a descendent of yours on the throne forever and that his reign will last for all time. Israel noticed soon enough that this did not have to do with the endurance of the Davidic line in history—since that line was broken at the Babylonian exile—but they preserved the hope nevertheless. In the opening chapter of the Gospel of Luke, we find the account of the Annunciation. The angel Gabriel tells the Virgin Mary that, through the power of the Holy Spirit, she will give birth to a son and that "he will be great, and will be called the Son of the Most High, and the Lord God will give to him the throne of his ancestor David. He will reign over the house of Jacob forever, and of his kingdom there will be no end" (Luke 1:32–33). This is nothing other than the announcement of the fulfillment of Nathan's prophecy that a definitive son of David would come, a *Mashiach* par excellence, the king and the priest, the Christ.

Reflection

St. Gregory Thaumaturgus
Homily

Today are strains of praise sung joyfully by the choir of angels, and the light of the advent of Christ shines brightly upon the faithful. Today is the glad springtime to us, and Christ the Sun of righteousness has beamed with clear light around us, and has illumined the minds of the faithful. Today is Adam made anew, and moves in the choir of angels, having winged his way to heaven. Today is the whole circle of the earth filled with joy, since the sojourn of the Holy Spirit has been realized to men. Today the grace of God and the hope of the unseen shine through all wonders transcending imagination, and make the mystery that was kept hidden from eternity plainly discernible to us. . . .

Today did Gabriel, who stands by God, come to the pure virgin, bearing to her the glad annunciation, "Hail, you that are highly favored! . . . And fear not, Mary; for I am not come to overpower you with fear, but to repel the subject of fear. Fear not, Mary, for you have found favor with God. Question not grace by the standard of nature. For grace does not endure to pass under the laws of nature. You know, O Mary, things kept hidden from the patriarchs and prophets. You have learned, O virgin, things which were kept concealed till now from the angels. You have heard, O purest one, things of which even the choir of inspired men was never deemed worthy. Moses, and David, and Isaiah, and Daniel, and all the prophets, prophesied of him; but the manner they knew not. Yet you alone, O purest virgin, are now made the recipient of things of which all these were kept in ignorance, and you learn the origin of them. For where the Holy Spirit is, there are all things readily ordered. Where divine grace is present, all things are found possible with God. The Holy Spirit shall come upon you, and the power of the highest shall overshadow you. Therefore also that holy thing which shall be born of you shall be called the Son of God."

Poem

Dante
From *Paradise*

"Virgin Mother, daughter of your Son,
    humbler and loftier past creation's measure,
    the fulcrum of the everlasting plan,
You are she who ennobled human nature
    so highly, that its Maker did not scorn
    to make Himself the Creature of His creature.
In your womb was the flame of love reborn,
    in the eternal peace of whose warm ray
    this flower has sprung and is so richly grown.
For us you are the torch of the noonday
    of charity; below, you are the spring
    of ever-living hope for men that die.
Lady, so great you are, such strength you bring,
    who does not run to you and looks for grace,
    his wish would seek to fly without a wing.
Not only does your kindness come to brace
    our courage when we beg: often your free
    favor arrives before our prayer's race.
In you is mercy, in you is piety,
    in you magnificence, in you the sum
    of excellence in all things that come to be."

Hymn

Alma Redemptoris Mater

Latin

Alma Redemptoris Mater, quae pervia caeli
Porta manes, et stella maris, succurre cadenti,
Surgere qui curat populo: tu quae genuisti,
Natura mirante, tuum sanctum Genitorem
Virgo prius ac posterius, Gabrielis ab ore
Sumens illud Ave, peccatorum miserere.

English

Loving mother of the Redeemer,
gate of heaven, star of the sea,
assist your people who have fallen yet strive to rise again.
To the wonderment of nature you bore your Creator,
yet remained a virgin after as before.
You who received Gabriel's joyful greeting,
have pity on us poor sinners.

Reflection
St. Bernard of Clairvaux
Homily

You have heard, O Virgin, that you will conceive and bear a son; you have heard that it will not be by man but by the Holy Spirit. The angel awaits an answer; it is time for him to return to God who sent him. We too are waiting, O Lady, for your word of compassion; the sentence of condemnation weighs heavily upon us.

The price of our salvation is offered to you. We shall be set free at once if you consent. In the eternal Word of God we all came to be, and behold, we die. In your brief response we are to be remade in order to be recalled to life.

Tearful Adam with his sorrowing family begs this of you, O loving Virgin, in their exile from Paradise. Abraham begs it, David begs it. All the other holy patriarchs, your ancestors, ask it of you, as they dwell in the country of the shadow of death. This is what the whole earth waits for, prostrate at your feet. It is right in doing so, for on your word depends comfort for the wretched, ransom for the captive, freedom for the condemned, indeed, salvation for all the sons of Adam, the whole of your race.

Answer quickly, O Virgin. Reply in haste to the angel, or rather through the angel to the Lord. Answer with a word, receive the Word of God. Speak your own word, conceive the divine Word. Breathe a passing word, embrace the eternal Word.

Why do you delay, why are you afraid? Believe, give praise, and receive. Let humility be bold, let modesty be confident. This is no time for virginal simplicity to forget prudence. In this matter alone, O prudent Virgin, do not fear to be presumptuous. Though modest silence is pleasing, dutiful speech is now more necessary. Open your heart to faith, O blessed Virgin, your lips to praise, your womb to the Creator. See, the desired of all nations is at your door, knocking to enter. If he should pass by because of your delay, in sorrow you would begin to seek him afresh, the One whom your soul loves. Arise, hasten, open. Arise in faith, hasten in devotion, open in praise and thanksgiving. "Behold the handmaid of the Lord," she says, "be it done to me according to your word."

Prayer
St. Teresa of Kolkata
The Co-Worker Newsletter

Mary, mother of Jesus, be a Mother to each of us, that we, like you, may be pure in heart; that we, like you, love Jesus; that we, like you, serve the poorest, for we are all poor.

Amen.

Poem

G.K. Chesterton
"Regina Angelorum"

Our Lady went into a strange country,
    Our Lady, for she was ours
And had run on the little hills behind the houses
    And pulled small flowers;
But she rose up and went into a strange country
    With strange thrones and powers.

And there were giants in the land she walked in,
    Tall as their toppling towns,
With heads so high in heaven, the constellations
    Served them for crowns;
And their feet might have forded like a brook the abysses
    Where Babel drowns.

They were girt about with the wings of the morning and
  evening
    Furled and unfurled,
Round the speckled sky where our small spinning planet
    Like a top is twirled;
And the swords they waved were the unending comets
    That shall end the world.

And moving in innocence and in accident,
    She turned the face
That none has ever looked on without loving
    On the Lords of Space;
And one hailed her with her name in our own country
    That is full of grace.

Our Lady went into a strange country
    And they crowned her for a queen,
For she needed never to be stayed or questioned
    But only seen;
And they were broken down under unbearable beauty
    As we have been.

But ever she walked till away in the last high places
    One great light shone
From the pillared throne of the king of all that country
    Who sat thereon;
And she cried aloud as she cried under the gibbet
    For she saw her son.

Our Lady wears a crown in a strange country,
    The crown he gave,
But she has not forgotten to call to her old companions,
    To call and crave;
And to hear her calling a man might arise and thunder
    On the doors of the grave.

"The knot of Eve's disobedience was loosed by the obedience of Mary. For what the virgin Eve had bound fast through unbelief, this did the virgin Mary set free through faith."

—ST. IRENAEUS

The Third
Week *of* Advent

THE
INCARNATION

Scripture
Luke 1:39–80

Mary set out and traveled to the hill country in haste to a town of Judah, where she entered the house of Zechariah and greeted Elizabeth. When Elizabeth heard Mary's greeting, the infant leaped in her womb, and Elizabeth, filled with the Holy Spirit, cried out in a loud voice and said, "Blessed are you among women, and blessed is the fruit of your womb. And how does this happen to me, that the mother of my Lord should come to me? For at the moment the sound of your greeting reached my ears, the infant in my womb leaped for joy. Blessed are you who believed that what was spoken to you by the Lord would be fulfilled."

And Mary said:

> "My soul proclaims the greatness of the Lord;
>> my spirit rejoices in God my Savior
>> for he has looked upon his lowly servant.
>
> From this day all generations will call me blessed:
>> the Almighty has done great things for me,
>> and holy is his Name.
>> He has mercy on those who fear him
>> in every generation.
>
> He has shown the strength of his arm,
>> and has scattered the proud in their conceit.

He has cast down the mighty from their thrones,
>   and has lifted up the lowly.

He has filled the hungry with good things,
>   and the rich he has sent away empty.

He has come to the help of his servant Israel
>   for he has remembered his promise of mercy,
>   the promise he made to our fathers,
>   to Abraham and his children for ever."

Mary remained with her about three months and then returned to her home.

When the time arrived for Elizabeth to have her child she gave birth to a son. Her neighbors and relatives heard that the Lord had shown his great mercy toward her, and they rejoiced with her. When they came on the eighth day to circumcise the child, they were going to call him Zechariah after his father, but his mother said in reply, "No. He will be called John." But they answered her, "There is no one among your relatives who has this name." So they made signs, asking his father what he wished him to be called. He asked for a tablet and wrote, "John is his name," and all were amazed. Immediately his mouth was opened, his tongue freed, and he spoke blessing God. Then fear came upon all their neighbors, and all these matters were discussed throughout the hill country of Judea. All who heard these things took them to heart, saying, "What, then, will this child be?" For surely the hand of the Lord was with him.

Zechariah his father, filled with the Holy Spirit, prophesied, saying:
"Blessed be the Lord, the God of Israel;
for he has come to his people and set them free.
He has raised up for us a mighty Savior,
born of the house of his servant David.
Through his prophets he promised of old
that he would save us from our enemies,
from the hands of all who hate us.
He promised to show mercy to our fathers
and to remember his holy covenant.
This was the oath he swore to our father Abraham:
to set us free from the hand of our enemies,
free to worship him without fear,
holy and righteous in his sight
all the days of our life.
You, my child, shall be called the prophet of the Most High,
for you will go before the Lord to prepare his way,
to give his people knowledge of salvation
by the forgiveness of their sins.
In the tender compassion of our God
the dawn from on high shall break upon us,

to shine on those who dwell in darkness and the
shadow of death,
and to guide our feet into the way of peace."

The child grew and became strong in spirit, and he was in
the desert until the day of his manifestation to Israel.

Reading

Bishop Barron
Catholicism

What is the Catholic thing? What makes Catholicism,
among all of the competing philosophies, ideologies, and
religions of the world, distinctive? I stand with St. John
Henry Newman, who said that the great principle of
Catholicism is the Incarnation, the enfleshment of God.
What do I mean by this? I mean the Word of God—the
mind by which the whole universe came to be—did not
remain sequestered in heaven, but rather entered into this
ordinary world of bodies, this grubby arena of history, this
compromised and tear-stained human condition of ours.
"The Word became flesh and made his dwelling among us"
(John 1:14): that is the Catholic thing.

The Incarnation tells central truths concerning both God
and us. If God became human without ceasing to be God and
without compromising the integrity of the creature that he

became, God must not be a competitor with his creation. In many of the ancient myths and legends, divine figures such as Zeus or Dionysus enter into human affairs only through aggression, destroying or wounding that which they invade. And in many of the philosophies of modernity, God is construed as a threat to human well-being. In their own ways, Marx, Freud, Feuerbach, and Sartre all maintain that God must be eliminated if humans are to be fully themselves. But there is none of this in the Christian doctrine of the Incarnation. The Word does indeed become human, but nothing of the human is destroyed in the process; God does indeed enter into his creation, but the world is thereby enhanced and elevated. The God capable of incarnation is not a competitive supreme being, but rather, in the words of St. Thomas Aquinas, the sheer act of being itself, that which grounds and sustains all of creation, the way a singer sustains a song.

And the Incarnation tells us the most important truth about ourselves: we are destined for divinization. The Church Fathers never tired of repeating this phrase as a sort of summary of Christian belief: *Deus fit homo ut homo fieret Deus* (God became human so that humans might become God). God condescended to enter into flesh so that our flesh might partake of the divine life, that we might participate in the love that holds the Father, Son, and Holy Spirit in communion. And this is why Christianity is the greatest humanism that has ever appeared, indeed that *could* ever appear. No philosophical or political or religious program in history—neither Greek nor Renaissance nor Marxist humanism—has ever made a claim about human destiny as extravagant as Christianity's. We are called not simply to moral perfection or artistic self-expression or economic liberation but to what the Eastern fathers called *theiosis*, transformation into God.

I realize that an objection might be forming in your mind. Certainly, the doctrine of the Incarnation separates Christianity from the other great world religions, but how does it distinguish Catholicism from the other Christian churches? Don't Protestants and the Orthodox hold just as firmly to the conviction that the Word became flesh? They do indeed, but they don't, I would argue, embrace the doctrine in its fullness. They don't see all the way to the bottom of it or draw out all of its implications. Essential to the Catholic mind is what I would characterize as a keen sense of the prolongation of the Incarnation throughout space and time, an extension that is made possible through the mystery of the Church. Catholics see God's continued enfleshment in the oil, water, bread, imposed hands, wine, and salt of the sacraments; they appreciate it in the gestures, movements, incensations, and songs of the liturgy; they savor it in the texts, arguments, and debates of the theologians; they sense it in the graced governance of popes and bishops; they love it in the struggles and missions of the saints; they know it in the writings of Catholic poets and in the cathedrals crafted by Catholic architects, artists, and workers. In short, all of this discloses to the Catholic eye and mind the ongoing presence of the Word made flesh—namely, Christ.

Newman said that a complex idea is equivalent to the sum total of its possible aspects. This means, he saw, that ideas are only really known across great stretches of space and time, with the gradual unfolding of their many dimensions and profiles. The Incarnation is one of the richest and most complex ideas ever proposed to the mind, and hence it demands the space and time of the Church in order fully to disclose itself. This is why, in order to grasp it fully, we have to read the Gospels, the epistles of Paul, the *Confessions* of St. Augustine, the *Summa theologiae* of Thomas Aquinas, the *Divine Comedy* of Dante, St. John of the Cross' *Ascent of Mount Carmel,* the *Story of a Soul* of Thérèse of Lisieux, among many other master texts. But we also have to *look and listen.* We must consult the Cathedral of Chartres, the Sainte-Chapelle, the Arena Chapel, the Sistine Chapel ceiling, Bernini's *Ecstasy of Saint Teresa,* the Church of the Holy Sepulchre, Grünewald's Crucifixion in the *Isenheim Altarpiece,* the soaring melodies of Gregorian chant, the Masses of Mozart, and the motets of Palestrina. Catholicism is a matter of the body and the senses as much as it is a matter of the mind and the soul, precisely because the Word became *flesh.*

Reflection

St. Athanasius

On the Incarnation of the Word

He was made man that we might be made God; and he
manifested himself by a body that we might receive the idea
of the unseen Father; and he endured the insolence of men
that we might inherit immortality. For while he himself
was in no way injured, being impassible and incorruptible
and very Word and God, men who were suffering, and
for whose sakes he endured all this, he maintained and
preserved in his own impassibility.

And, in a word, the achievements of the Savior, resulting
from his becoming man, are of such kind and number, that
if one should wish to enumerate them, he may be compared
to men who gaze at the expanse of the sea and wish to count
its waves. For as one cannot take in the whole of the waves
with his eyes, for those which are coming on baffle the sense
of him that attempts it; so for him that would take in all the
achievements of Christ in the body, it is impossible to take
in the whole, even by reckoning them up, as those which
go beyond his thought are more than those he thinks he
has taken in.

Better is it, then, not to aim at speaking of the whole,
where one cannot do justice even to a part, but, after
mentioning one more, to leave the whole for you to marvel

at. For all alike are marvelous, and wherever a man turns his glance, he may behold on that side the divinity of the Word, and be struck with exceeding great awe.

Poem

St. John of the Cross
From "Ballad on the Gospel"

Now that the season had arrived
Appointed long ago
For the ransom of the Bride, who served
Beneath a heavy yoke,

According to the ancient law
Which Moses laid upon her,
The Father moved with tender love
To this effect then spoke:

    My Son, you see now that your Bride
In your image has been formed,
And where she most resembles you,
You both are in accord.

But she differs through the flesh,
Not found in your pure soul;
There is, for love's perfection,
A law of love to know:

That the lover take on likeness
To the loved one of his heart,
And the closer the resemblance
The greater the delight.

And this delight within your Bride
Would greatly be increased,
If the flesh she is endowed with
She saw you also shared.

My will is yours and yours alone,
The Son to him replied,
The sovereign glory I possess
Is that your will be mine.

So I accord with you, my Father,
In everything you say.
Your loving kindness will be seen
More clearly in this way.

Your mightiness and wisdom
And justice will be shown.
I shall go and tell the world
And make the tidings known
Of your graciousness and beauty
And of your sovereign throne.

I shall go and seek my Bride,
And I myself will bear
The weariness and hardship
That submerge her life in care.

And so that she may have life
I shall die for her sake,
And to you again restore her,
Lifted from the lake.

Hymn

Rorate Caeli

Latin

Rorate caeli desuper, et nubes pluant iustum.

Ne irascaris Domine, ne ultra memineris iniquitatis:
Ecce civitas Sancti facta est deserta:
Sion deserta facta est: Ierusalem desolata est:
Domus sanctificationis tuae et gloriae tuae,
Ubi laudaverunt te patres nostri.
(REFRAIN)

Peccavimus, et facti sumus tamquam immundus nos,
Et cecidimus quasi folium universi:
Et iniquitatis nostrae quasi ventus abstulerunt nos:
Abscondisti faciem tuam a nobis,
Et allisisti nos in manu iniquitatis nostrae.
(REFRAIN)

English

You heavens, open from above, that clouds may rain down
the Just One.

Do not be angry, Lord our God,
No longer be mindful that we have sinned before you.
See how Zion, your city, now is left abandoned.
Zion is left unguarded now, Jerusalem now is desolate:
City that claimed your loving blessing and worked for your glory,
City where your fathers sang your praises.
(REFRAIN)

We know our sin, and we are burdened as with
    some loathsome thing,
And have fallen down just like leaves in the blast of winter:
And the sins we have committed just like winds
    have blown us all about.
You have taken from us your brightness and comfort,
And you have broken us by laying the debt of our sins upon us.
(REFRAIN)

51

Vide, Domine, afflictionem populi tui,
Et mitte quem missurus es:
Emitte Agnum dominatorem terrae,
De petra deserti ad montem filiae Sion:
Ut auferat ipse iugum captivitatis nostrae.
(REFRAIN)

Consolamini, consolamini, popule meus:
Cito veniet salus tua:
Quare maerore consumeris, quia innovavit te dolor?
Salvabo te, noli timere, ego enim sum Dominus Deus tuus,
Sanctus Israel, Redemptor tuus.
(REFRAIN)

Lord, now turn to us and see your chosen people's affliction
And send down him who is to come,
The one promised, Lamb and yet Lord of all lands,
From the rock in the desert to the mount of Zion, your daughter,
That he may bring pardon, freeing us captives of our burden.
(REFRAIN)

Be you comforted, be you comforted, hear me, my people:
Soon shall come to you Christ, your Savior.
Why do you give way to sorrowing:
Has this grieving ended your sadness?
Your Savior comes, do not be fearful, for it is I,
    your God and mighty Ruler,
Zion's Holy One and your Redeemer.
(REFRAIN)

Reflection
St. Bonaventure
The Tree of Life

Jesus Prefigured

At the beginning of the creation of nature, our first parents were placed in paradise; but they were driven out by the severity of God's decree because they ate of the forbidden tree. From that time his heavenly mercy has not ceased calling straying man back to the way of penance by giving hope of forgiveness and by promising that a Savior would come. Lest such condescension on God's part should fail to effect our salvation because of ignorance and ingratitude, he never ceased announcing, promising, and prefiguring the coming of his Son in the five ages of history, through the patriarchs, judges, priests, kings, and prophets, from Abel the Just to John the Baptist. Through many thousands of years, by many marvelous prophecies he stirred men's minds to faith and inflamed their hearts with living desires.

Jesus Sent from Heaven
(see Matt. 1:18–23; Luke 1:26–38)

Finally, the *fullness of time* (Gal. 4:4) had come. . . . The Archangel Gabriel was sent to the Virgin. When she gave her consent to him, the Holy Spirit came upon her like a divine fire inflaming her soul and sanctifying her flesh in perfect purity. But the *power of the Most High overshadowed* her (Luke 1:35) so that she could endure such fire. By the action of that power, instantly his body was formed, his soul created, and at once both were united to the divinity in the Person of the Son, so that the same Person was God and man, with the properties of each nature maintained.

Oh, if you could feel in some way
the quality and intensity of that fire sent from heaven,
the refreshing coolness that accompanied it,
the consolation it imparted;
if you could realize the great exaltation of the Virgin Mother,
the ennobling of the human race,
the condescension of the divine majesty;
if you could hear the Virgin singing with joy;
if you could go with your Lady
into the mountainous region;
if you could see the sweet embrace
of the Virgin and the woman who had been sterile
and hear the greeting
in which the tiny servant recognized his Lord,
the herald his Judge
and the voice his Word,
then I am sure

you would sing in sweet tones
with the Blessed Virgin
that sacred hymn:
"My soul magnifies the Lord" (Luke 1:46) . . . ;
and with the tiny prophet
you would exalt, rejoice, and adore
the marvelous virginal conception!

Prayer
St. Catherine of Siena
The Dialogue

My Lord, turn the eye of your mercy on your people and on your mystic body, holy Church. . . .

You said, "Let us make humankind in our image and likeness" (Gen. 1:26). And this you did, eternal Trinity, willing that we should share all that you are, high eternal Trinity! You, eternal Father, gave us memory to hold your gifts and share your power. You gave us understanding so that, seeing your goodness, we might share the wisdom of your only-begotten Son. And you gave us free will to love what our understanding sees and knows of your truth, and so share the mercy of your Holy Spirit.

Why did you so dignify us? With unimaginable love you looked upon your creatures within your very self, and you fell in love with us. So it was love that made you create us and give us being, just so that we might taste your supreme eternal good.

Then I see how by our sin we lost the dignity you had given us. Rebels that we were, we declared war on your mercy and became your enemies. But stirred by the same fire that made you create us, you decided to give this warring human race a way to reconciliation, bringing great peace out of our war. So you gave us your only-begotten Son, your Word, to be mediator between us and you. He became our justice (1 Cor. 1:30) taking on himself the punishment for our injustices. He offered you the obedience you required of him in clothing him with our humanity, eternal Father, taking on our likeness and our human nature!

O depth of love! What heart could keep from breaking at the sight of your greatness descending to the lowliness of our humanity? We are your image, and now by making yourself one with us you have become our image, veiling your eternal divinity in the wretched cloud and dung heap of Adam. And why? For love! You, God, became human and we have been made divine! In the name of this unspeakable love, then, I beg you—I would force you even!—to have mercy on your creatures.

Amen.

Poem

G.K. Chesterton
"Gloria in Profundis"

There has fallen on earth for a token
A god too great for the sky.
He has burst out of all things and broken
The bounds of eternity:
Into time and the terminal land
He has strayed like a thief or a lover,
For the wine of the world brims over,
Its splendour is split on the sand.

Who is proud when the heavens are humble,
Who mounts if the mountains fall,
If the fixed suns topple and tumble
And a deluge of love drowns all—
Who rears up his head for a crown,
Who holds up his will for a warrant,
Who strives with the starry torrent,
When all that is good goes down?

For in dread of such falling and failing
The Fallen Angels fell
Inverted in insolence, scaling
The hanging mountain of hell:

But unmeasured of plummet and rod
Too deep for their sight to scan,
Outrushing the fall of man
Is the height of the fall of God.

Glory to God in the Lowest
The spout of the stars in spate—
Where thunderbolt thinks to be slowest
And the lightning fears to be late:
As men dive for sunken gem
Pursuing, we hunt and hound it,
The fallen star has found it
In the cavern of Bethlehem.

"God is pure Spirit but our salvation was accomplished when the Spirit was made flesh."

—FLANNERY O'CONNOR

The Fourth
Week *of* Advent

THE JOURNEY TO
BETHLEHEM

Scripture
Luke 2:1–7

In those days a decree went out from Caesar Augustus that the whole world should be enrolled. This was the first enrollment, when Quirinius was governor of Syria. So all went to be enrolled, each to his own town. And Joseph too went up from Galilee from the town of Nazareth to Judea, to the city of David that is called Bethlehem, because he was of the house and family of David, to be enrolled with Mary, his betrothed, who was with child. While they were there, the time came for her to have her child, and she gave birth to her firstborn son.

Reading

Bishop Barron
Light from Light

In many ways, the entire Bible is a book of battles. I am
not speaking simply of the many military conflicts narrated
therein; I am speaking of the almost constant struggle
between the ways and purposes of God and those forces
that stand opposed to the divine intention. From the
opening lines of the Scriptures, we find the Spirit of God
drawing life and order from the *tohu wabohu*, the watery
chaos. Even in the Garden of Eden, we find the serpent,
indeed the cleverest of God's creatures, but also a source of
tremendous mischief. In the wake of original sin, Adam
and Eve fall into conflict with one another and with the
realm of nature. Cain hates his brother and murders him.
By the time of Noah, sin had become so pervasive that the
tohu wabohu returns in the form of an all-destroying flood.

Once established through a series of covenants, the holy
people Israel is opposed on every front and from within.
The Egyptians enslave Israel; Amalek and Philistia harass
it; every power in the Promised Land stands opposed to it;
Assyria, Persia, Babylon, Greece, and Rome conquer it. Its
most sacred artifacts are destroyed; the temple itself, the
dwelling of God on earth, is burned to the ground. And
from the inside, Israel is constantly threatened as well: the

sins of her own people, civil war, kingly rivalry, stupidity, resentment, violence, cruelty, the wanton disregard of the commandments of the Lord, the worship of false gods. In his magnificent homilies on the book of Exodus, Origen of Alexandria construes Israel as representative of all of those energies and instincts congruent with the will of God, and the Egyptians as symbolic of all of those forces opposed to God. How tragically telling, he observes, that Egypt has enslaved Israel, meaning that what is best in ourselves and in our societies is often in thrall to what is worst in ourselves and our societies. The Israelite slaves are compelled by their masters to build monuments and fortified cities for their oppressors; indeed, our intelligence, creativity, and energy are dedicated to the building of monuments to and fortifications for our selfishness, violence, and idolatry. Almost invariably, when God's spokespersons and representatives come on the scene, they are met with opposition. Think of the Israelites grumbling against Moses, or of the fierce military opposition faced by Joshua, or of Saul's deep resentment and constant harassment of David, or of the murderous opponents of Jeremiah the prophet, or of the Babylonian invaders who carried the prophet Ezekiel away.

All of this comes to full expression in the New Testament. From the very commencement of his life, Jesus, the one who speaks and acts in the very person of God, is opposed. When we read the familiar Lukan Christmas account through the right interpretive lenses, we see that it is far from a charming story that one might recite to children. Instead, it is marked, through and through, by the themes of conflict and opposition. The tale opens in the way that one might expect, by invoking great and mighty figures: Quirinius, the Roman governor of Syria, and Caesar Augustus, who effectively ruled the world. But Luke turns our expectations upside down when he makes it clear whom the narrative is about: not Caesar and Quirinius, but two obscure figures making their way to Bethlehem, prompted by Caesar's imperious call for a census of the whole world. The baby to whom the woman is about to give birth is the focus of Luke's attention.

We must read the account, in point of fact, as a contrast between two ideas of kingship. The baby is born in a cave or a stable and placed in a dirty trough where animals eat. The best protected and best fed person in the ancient world would have been Caesar, and such advantages are normally seen as perquisites of the powerful. The baby is wrapped up in swaddling clothes, rendering him utterly incapable of movement. The most mobile and rangy person in the ancient world would have been Caesar Augustus, able to accomplish practically anything he wanted, and such a capacity is normally appreciated as a mark of the good life. Caesar had an enormous army, which is why he was capable of dominating his world. But the baby king, we discover, is the commander of a *stratias* (army) of angels, and this provides the hermeneutical key to the narrative. True world-conquering power is associated with humility, love, nonviolence, and poverty, not with the qualities valued by a fallen world. The Lukan Christmas story is something like an operatic overture, since it anticipates the central theme that will mark almost every aspect of the coming drama. Two kings, two ideas of kingship, two rival conceptions of power will battle against one another throughout the Gospel, and the *point* of the story is that one of them wins out.

Reflection
Pope Benedict XVI
Jesus of Nazareth: The Infancy Narratives

For the first time, "all the world" (Luke 2:1), the *ecumēnē* in its entirety, is to be enrolled. For the first time there is a government and an empire that spans the globe. For the first time, there is a great expanse of peace in which everyone's property can be registered and placed at the service of the wider community. Only now, when there is a commonality of law and property on a large scale, and when a universal language has made it possible for a cultural community to trade in ideas and goods, only now can a message of universal salvation, a universal Savior, enter the world: it is indeed the "fullness of time." . . .

It was not with the timelessness of myth that Jesus came to be born among us. He belongs to a time that can be precisely dated and a geographical area that is precisely defined: here the universal and the concrete converge. It was in him that the *Lógos*, the creative logic behind all things, entered the world. The eternal *Lógos* became man: the context of place and time is part of this. Faith attaches itself to this concrete reality.

Poem
Gerard Manley Hopkins
"Moonless Darkness"

Moonless darkness stands between.
Past, the Past, no more be seen!
But the Bethlehem-star may lead me
To the sight of Him who freed me
From the self that I have been.
Make me pure, Lord: thou art holy;
Make me meek, Lord: thou wert lowly;
Now beginning, and alway:
Now begin, on Christmas Day.

Hymn

O Magnum Mysterium

Latin

O magnum mysterium,
et admirabile sacramentum,
ut animalia viderent Dominum natum,
iacentum in praesepio:
Beata Virgo, cuius viscera
meruerunt portare
Dominum Iesum Christum.
Alleluia!

English

O great mystery,
and wonderful sacrament,
that animals should see the Lord born,
lying in a crib;
O Blessed Virgin, whose womb
was deemed worthy to bear
the Lord Jesus Christ.
Alleluia!

Reflection

St. Thomas Aquinas

Summa theologiae

It is written (Mic. 5:2): "And you, Bethlehem, Ephrata . . . out of you shall he come forth unto me, that is to be the ruler in Israel." . . .

Christ willed to be born in Bethlehem for two reasons. First, because "he was made . . . of the seed of David according to the flesh," as it is written (Rom. 1:3); to whom also was a special promise made concerning Christ; according to 2 Samuel 23:1: "The man to whom it was appointed concerning the Christ of the God of Jacob . . . said." Therefore he willed to be born at Bethlehem, where David was born, in order that by the very birthplace the promise made to David might be shown to be fulfilled. The Evangelist points this out by saying: "Because he was of the house and of the family of David." Secondly, because, as Gregory says (*Hom. viii in Evang.*): "Bethlehem is interpreted 'the house of bread.' It is Christ himself who said, 'I am the living Bread which came down from heaven.'"

Prayer

Pope Francis
Patris Corde

Hail, Guardian of the Redeemer,
Spouse of the Blessed Virgin Mary.
To you God entrusted his only Son;
in you Mary placed her trust;
with you Christ became man.

Blessed Joseph, to us too,
show yourself a father
and guide us in the path of life.
Obtain for us grace, mercy, and courage,
and defend us from every evil.
Amen.

Poem

G.K. Chesterton
"The House of Christmas"

There fared a mother driven forth
Out of an inn to roam;
In the place where she was homeless
All men are at home.
The crazy stable close at hand,
With shaking timber and shifting sand,
Grew a stronger thing to abide and stand
Than the square stones of Rome.

For men are homesick in their homes,
And strangers under the sun,
And they lay on their heads in a foreign land
Whenever the day is done.
Here we have battle and blazing eyes,
And chance and honour and high surprise,
But our homes are under miraculous skies
Where the yule tale was begun.

A Child in a foul stable,
Where the beasts feed and foam;
Only where He was homeless
Are you and I at home;

We have hands that fashion and heads that know,
But our hearts we lost—how long ago!
In a place no chart nor ship can show
Under the sky's dome.

This world is wild as an old wives' tale,
And strange the plain things are,
The earth is enough and the air is enough
For our wonder and our war;
But our rest is as far as the fire-drake swings
And our peace is put in impossible things
Where clashed and thundered unthinkable wings
Round an incredible star.

To an open house in the evening
Home shall men come,
To an older place than Eden
And a taller town than Rome.
To the end of the way of the wandering star,
To the things that cannot be and that are,
To the place where God was homeless
And all men are at home.

"He chose both a poor mother, from whom he was born, and a poor homeland, about which it is said, 'And you, Bethlehem, you are the least among the tribes of Judah' (Mic. 5:2)."

—ORIGEN

Christmas Day

THE NATIVITY

Scripture
John 1:1–18

In the beginning was the Word,
    and the Word was with God,
    and the Word was God.
He was in the beginning with God.
All things came to be through him,
    and without him nothing came to be.
What came to be through him was life,
    and this life was the light of the human race;
the light shines in the darkness,
    and the darkness has not overcome it.
A man named John was sent from God. He came for testimony, to testify to the light, so that all might believe through him. He was not the light, but came to testify to the light. The true light, which enlightens everyone, was coming into the world.

  He was in the world,
    and the world came to be through him,
    but the world did not know him.
  He came to what was his own,
    but his own people did not accept him.
But to those who did accept him he gave power to become children of God, to those who believe in his name, who were born not by natural generation nor by human choice

nor by a man's decision but of God.

And the Word became flesh
and made his dwelling among us,
and we saw his glory,
the glory as of the Father's only Son,
full of grace and truth.

John testified to him and cried out, saying, "This was he of whom I said, 'The one coming after me ranks ahead of me because he existed before me.'" From his fullness we have all received, grace in place of grace, because while the law was given through Moses, grace and truth came through Jesus Christ. No one has ever seen God. The only-begotten Son, God, who is at the Father's side, has revealed him.

Reading

Bishop Barron
Vibrant Paradoxes

One of the most magnificent passages in the Scriptures, indeed one of the gems of the Western literary tradition, is the prologue to the Gospel of John. In many ways, the essential meaning of Christmas is contained in these elegantly crafted lines.

John commences: "In the beginning was the Word . . . " No first-century Jew would have missed the significance of that opening phrase, for the first word of the Hebrew Scriptures, *bereshit*, means precisely "beginning." The evangelist is signaling that the story he will unfold is the tale of a new creation, a new beginning. The Word, he tells us, was not only with God from the beginning, but indeed was God. Whenever we use words, we express something of ourselves. For example, as I type these words, I'm telling you what I know about the prologue to the Johannine Gospel; when you speak to a friend, you're telling him or her how you feel or what you're afraid of; when an umpire shouts out a call, he's communicating how he has assessed a play; etc. But God, the sheer act of being itself, the perfect Creator of the universe, is able utterly to speak himself in one great Word, a Word that does not simply contain an aspect of his being, but rather the whole of his being. This is why we say that the Word is "God from God, Light from Light, true God from true God"; and this is why St. John says that the Word was God.

Then we hear that through this Word "all things came to be." The Logos of God would necessarily contain the fullness of rationality and order, for he is nothing other than the mind of God. Hence, when the Father made the universe, he "consulted" the Son, the way that an artist might consult a preliminary draft or an architect a diagram. The Word is the prototype in which all forms of reasonable structure are implicitly present. And this is precisely why the universe is not dumbly there but intelligibly there, why it is marked, in every nook and cranny, by reasonability. This mystical theology of creation through the Word is one of the conditions for the possibility of the physical sciences, for every scientist must assume the intelligibility of what she investigates.

Next, we are told of a man "sent from God" whose name was John. The Baptist came, St. John tells us, "for testimony, to testify to the light," for he was not, himself, the light. From time immemorial, God has sent messengers, spokespersons. Think of all of the prophets and patriarchs of Israel, indeed of every sage, philosopher, artist, or poet who has communicated something of God's truth and beauty. All of these could be characterized as witnesses to the light. The point is that the one to whom the Baptist bears witness is someone qualitatively different, not one more bearer of the

Word, however impressive, but the Word himself. What is being held off here is the tendency—as prevalent today as in the ancient world—to domesticate Jesus and turn him into one more in a long line of prophets and seers.

"He was in the world, and the world came to be through him, but the world did not know him." In that pithily crafted line, we sense the whole tragedy of sin. Human beings were made by and for the Logos, and therefore they find their joy in a sort of sympathetic attunement to the Logos. Sin is the disharmony that comes when we fall out of alignment with God's reasonable purpose. But then comes the incomparably good news: "But to those who did accept him he gave power to become children of God." It is a basic principle of nature that nothing at a lower level of being can rise to a higher level unless it is drawn upward. A chemical can become part of a more complex structure only if it is assimilated by a plant; a plant can become ingredient in a sentient nature only if it is devoured by an animal; an animal can participate in rationality only if it is taken in by a human being. By this same principle, a human being can become something higher, not through his own efforts, but only when a superior reality assimilates him. The Church Fathers consistently taught that God became human so that humans might become God—which is to say, participants in the divine nature. In a word, we can become children of God precisely because God reached down to us and became a son of man.

The entire prologue comes to its climax with the magnificent phrase "The Word became flesh and made his dwelling among us." The Gnostic temptation has tugged at the Church, on and off, for nearly the past two thousand years. This is the suggestion, common to all forms of puritanism, that the spiritual is attained through a negation of the material. But authentic Christianity, inspired by this stunning claim of St. John, has consistently held off Gnosticism, for it knows that the Word of God took to himself a human nature and thereby elevated all of matter and made it a sacrament of the divine presence.

The Greek phrase behind "made his dwelling among us" is literally translated as "tabernacled among us" or "pitched his tent among us." No Jew of John's time would have missed the wonderful connection implied between Jesus and the temple. According to the book of Exodus, the ark of the covenant—the embodiment of Yahweh's presence—was originally housed in a tent or tabernacle. The evangelist is telling us that now, in the flesh of Jesus, Yahweh has established his definitive tabernacle among us.

All of this sublime theology is John the Evangelist's great Christmas sermon. I would invite you to return to it often this season in prayer and meditation.

Reflection

G.K. Chesterton

The Everlasting Man

This sketch of the human story began in a cave; the cave which popular science associates with the caveman and in which practical discovery has really found archaic drawings of animals. The second half of human history, which was like a new creation of the world, also begins in a cave. There is even a shadow of such a fancy in the fact that animals were again present; for it was a cave used as a stable by the mountaineers of the uplands about Bethlehem; who still drive their cattle into such holes and caverns at night. It was here that a homeless couple had crept underground with the cattle when the doors of the crowded caravanserai had been shut in their faces; and it was here beneath the very feet of the passers-by, in a cellar under the very floor of the world, that Jesus Christ was born. But in that second creation there was indeed something symbolical in the roots of the primeval rock or the horns of the prehistoric herd. God also was a caveman, and had also traced strange shapes of creatures, curiously colored, upon the wall of the world; but the pictures that he made had come to life.

A mass of legend and literature, which increases and will never end, has repeated and rung the changes on that single paradox; that the hands that had made the sun and stars were too small to reach the huge heads of the cattle. Upon this paradox, we might almost say upon this jest, all the literature of our faith is founded. . . .

Any agnostic or atheist whose childhood has known a real Christmas has ever afterwards, whether he likes it or not, an association in his mind between two ideas that most of mankind must regard as remote from each other; the idea of a baby and the idea of unknown strength that sustains the stars. His instincts and imagination can still connect them, when his reason can no longer see the need of the connection; for him there will always be some savor of religion about the mere picture of a mother and a baby; some hint of mercy and softening about the mere mention of the dreadful name of God. . . . Omnipotence and impotence, or divinity and infancy, do definitely make a sort of epigram which a million repetitions cannot turn into a platitude. It is not unreasonable to call it unique. Bethlehem is emphatically a place where extremes meet. . . .

It might be suggested, in a somewhat violent image, that nothing had happened in that fold or crack in the great grey hills except that the whole universe had been turned inside out. I mean that all the eyes of wonder and worship which had been turned outwards to the largest thing were now turned inward to the smallest.

Poem

St. Thérèse of Lisieux

From "The Little Divine Beggar of Christmas"

All the earth with snow is covered,
 Everywhere the white frosts reign;
Winter and his gloomy courtiers
 Hold their court on earth again.
But for you has bloomed *the Flower*
 Of the fields, Who comes to earth
From the fatherland of heaven,
 Where eternal spring has birth.
Near the Rose of Christmas, Sister!
 In the lowly grasses hide,
And be like the humble flowerets,—
 Of heaven's King the lowly bride!

Day by day, at morn and even,
 Still the holy words are said:
O our Father up in Heaven!
 Give to us our daily bread,
Yet your God, become your Brother,
 Suffers hunger as you do;
And His childish voice is asking
 For *a little bread* from you.

Ah! my Sister! Jesus wishes
>Just your love,—how great your bliss!
Let your soul be pure and spotless,
>For *His daily bread is* this. . . .

Our sweet Jesus, Fire of love,
Light and Warmth of heaven above,
>In the stable, cold is He!
>Yet, in the far, shining sky,
Angels, living flames on high,
>Wait on Him in ecstasy.

Here on earth 'tis you must light
Blazing fires of love to-night,
>In your heart, all free from sin;
>Little shivering Jesus warm
In the shelter of your arm,
>By the souls your prayers shall win!

Hymn
Adeste Fidelis

Latin

Adeste, fideles,
Laeti triumphantes;
Venite, venite in Bethlehem;
Natum videte
Regem Angelorum:

REFRAIN:
Venite adoremus (3×)
Dominum.

Deum de Deo,
Lumen de Lumine,
Gestant puellae viscera,
Deum verum,
Genitum non factum.
(REFRAIN)

English

O come, all ye faithful,
Joyful and triumphant,
O come ye, O come ye to Bethlehem;
Come and behold him
Born the King of Angels:

REFRAIN:
O come, let us adore him (3×)
Christ the Lord.

God of God eternal,
Light from Light proceeding,
Lo, he deigns in the Virgin's womb to lie;
God uncreated,
Very God begotten.
(REFRAIN)

Cantet nunc Io
Chorus Angelorum;
Cantet nunc aula caelestium,
Gloria in excelsis Deo:
(REFRAIN)

Ergo qui natus
Die hodierna.
Iesu, tibi sit gloria,
Patris aeterni
Verbum caro factum.
(REFRAIN)

Sing, choirs of angels,
Sing in exultation,
Sing, all ye citizens of heaven above,
Glory to God in the highest:
(REFRAIN)

Yea, Lord, we greet thee,
Born this happy morning;
Jesus, to thee be glory given;
Word of the Father,
Now in flesh appearing.
(REFRAIN)

Reflection

St. Augustine
Sermon

Awake, mankind! For your sake God has become man. "Awake, you who sleep, rise up from the dead, and Christ will enlighten you" (Eph. 5:14). I tell you again: for your sake, God became man.

You would have suffered eternal death, had he not been born in time. Never would you have been freed from sinful flesh, had he not taken on himself the likeness of sinful flesh. You would have suffered everlasting unhappiness, had it not been for this mercy. You would never have returned to life, had he not shared your death. You would have been lost if he had not hastened to your aid. You would have perished, had he not come.

Let us then joyfully celebrate the coming of our salvation and redemption. Let us celebrate the festive day on which he who is the great and eternal day came from the great and endless day of eternity into our own short day of time.

"He has become our justice, our sanctification, our redemption, so that, as it is written: Let him who glories glory in the Lord" (1 Cor. 1:30–31).

"Truth, then, has arisen from the earth" (Ps. 85:11): Christ who said, "I am the Truth" (John 14:6), was born of a virgin. "And justice looked down from heaven" (Ps. 85:11):

because believing in this newborn child, man is justified not by himself but by God.

"Truth has arisen from the earth": because "the Word was made flesh" (John 1:14). "And justice looked down from heaven": because "every good gift and every perfect gift is from above" (James 1:17).

"Truth has arisen from the earth": flesh from Mary. "And justice looked down from heaven": for "man can receive nothing unless it has been given him from heaven" (John 3:27).

"Justified by faith, let us be at peace with God" (Rom. 5:1): for "justice and peace have embraced one another" (Ps. 85:10). "Through our Lord Jesus Christ": for "Truth has arisen from the earth." "Through whom we have access to that grace in which we stand, and our boast is in our hope of God's glory" (Rom. 5:1–2). He does not say: "of our glory," but "of God's glory": for "justice" has not proceeded from us but has "looked down from heaven." Therefore "he who glories, let him glory," not in himself, but "in the Lord."

For this reason, when our Lord was born of the Virgin, the message of the angelic voices was: "Glory to God in the highest, and peace to his people on earth" (Luke 2:14).

For how could there be peace on earth unless "Truth has arisen from the earth," that is, unless Christ were born of our flesh? And "he is our peace who made the two into one" (Eph. 2:14): that we might be men of good will, sweetly linked by the bond of unity.

Let us then rejoice in this grace, so that our glorying may bear witness to our good conscience by which we glory, not in ourselves, but in the Lord. That is why Scripture says: "He is my glory, the one who lifts up my head" (Ps. 3:3). For what greater grace could God have made to dawn on us than to make his only Son become the son of man, so that a son of man might in his turn become the son of God?

Ask if this were merited; ask for its reason, for its justification, and see whether you will find any other answer but sheer grace.

Prayer
Pope St. John XXIII
Journal of a Soul

O sweet Child of Bethlehem, grant that we may share with all our hearts in this profound mystery of Christmas. Put into the hearts of men this peace for which they sometimes seek so desperately and which you alone can give to them. Help them to know one another better, and to live as brothers, children of the same Father.

Reveal to them also your beauty, holiness, and purity. Awaken in their hearts love and gratitude for your infinite goodness. Join them all together in your love. And give us your heavenly peace.

Amen.

Poem

G.K. Chesterton
"A Xmas Carol"

The Christ-child lay on Mary's lap
    His hair was like a light
(O Weary Weary were the world
    But here is all aright)

The Christ-child lay on Mary's breast
    His hair was like a star
(O stern and cunning are the Kings
    But here the true hearts are)

The Christ-child lay on Mary's heart
    His hair was like a fire
(O Weary Weary is the World
    But here the world's desire)

The Christ-child stood on Mary's knee
    His hair was like a crown
And all the flowers looked up at him
    And all the stars looked down.

"Long ago God spoke to our ancestors in many and various ways by the prophets, but in these last days he has spoken to us by a Son."

—HEBREWS 1:1–2

The Christmas Season

THE HOLY FAMILY

Scripture
Luke 2:7–52

She wrapped him in swaddling clothes and laid him in a manger, because there was no room for them in the inn.

Now there were shepherds in that region living in the fields and keeping the night watch over their flock. The angel of the Lord appeared to them and the glory of the Lord shone around them, and they were struck with great fear. The angel said to them, "Do not be afraid; for behold, I proclaim to you good news of great joy that will be for all the people. For today in the city of David a savior has been born for you who is Christ and Lord. And this will be a sign for you: you will find an infant wrapped in swaddling clothes and lying in a manger." And suddenly there was a multitude of the heavenly host with the angel, praising God and saying:

"Glory to God in the highest
and on earth peace to those on whom his favor rests."

When the angels went away from them to heaven, the shepherds said to one another, "Let us go, then, to Bethlehem to see this thing that has taken place, which the Lord has made known to us." So they went in haste and found Mary and Joseph, and the infant lying in the manger. When they saw this, they made known the message that had been told them about this child. All who heard it were amazed by what had been told them by the shepherds. And Mary kept all these things, reflecting on them in her heart. Then the shepherds returned, glorifying and praising God for all they had heard and seen, just as it had been told to them.

When eight days were completed for his circumcision, he was named Jesus, the name given him by the angel before he was conceived in the womb.

When the days were completed for their purification according to the law of Moses, they took him up to Jerusalem to present him to the Lord, just as it is written in the law of the Lord, *Every male that opens the womb shall be consecrated to the Lord*, and to offer the sacrifice of *a pair of turtledoves or two young pigeons*, in accordance with the dictate in the law of the Lord.

Now there was a man in Jerusalem whose name was Simeon. This man was righteous and devout, awaiting the consolation of Israel, and the Holy Spirit was upon him. It had been revealed to him by the Holy Spirit that he should not see death before he had seen the Christ of the Lord. He came in the Spirit into the temple; and when the parents brought in the child Jesus to perform the custom of the law in regard to him, he took him into his arms and blessed God, saying:

"Now, Master, you may let your servant go
    in peace, according to your word,
for my eyes have seen your salvation,
    which you prepared in sight of all the peoples,
a light for revelation to the Gentiles,
    and glory for your people Israel."

The child's father and mother were amazed at what was said about him; and Simeon blessed them and said to Mary his mother, "Behold, this child is destined for the fall and rise of many in Israel, and to be a sign that will be contradicted—and you yourself a sword will pierce—so that the thoughts of many hearts may be revealed." There was also a prophetess, Anna, the daughter of Phanuel, of the tribe of Asher. She was advanced in years, having lived seven years with her husband after her marriage, and then as a widow until she was eighty-four. She never left the temple, but worshiped night and day with fasting and prayer. And coming forward at that very time, she gave thanks to God and spoke about the child to all who were awaiting the redemption of Jerusalem.

When they had fulfilled all the prescriptions of the law of the Lord, they returned to Galilee, to their own town of

Nazareth. The child grew and became strong, filled with wisdom; and the favor of God was upon him.

Each year Jesus' parents went to Jerusalem for the feast of Passover, and when he was twelve years old, they went up according to festival custom. After they had completed its days, as they were returning, the boy Jesus remained behind in Jerusalem, but his parents did not know it. Thinking that he was in the caravan, they journeyed for a day and looked for him among their relatives and acquaintances, but not finding him, they returned to Jerusalem to look for him. After three days they found him in the temple, sitting in the midst of the teachers, listening to them and asking them questions, and all who heard him were astounded at his understanding and his answers. When his parents saw him, they were astonished, and his mother said to him, "Son, why have you done this to us? Your father and I have been looking for you with great anxiety." And he said to them, "Why were you looking for me? Did you not know that I must be in my Father's house?" But they did not understand what he said to them. He went down with them and came to Nazareth, and was obedient to them; and his mother kept all these things in her heart. And Jesus advanced in wisdom and age and favor before God and man.

Reading

Bishop Barron
Proclaiming the Power of Christ

There are family values on display in the Bible, but they're probably not the ones you'd expect. We tend to be rather sentimental in regard to families, emphasizing the importance of emotional connections and personal bonds. But the biblical authors urge us to see the "values" of a family in an entirely different way. Unlike what we've come to expect, their approach is not romantic at all, but rather harsh, blunt, and demanding.

A particularly illuminating case in point is the story of Hannah, told in the first chapter of the first book of Samuel (1 Sam. 1:9–28). We are told that the childless Hannah would go every year up to the temple at Shiloh to pray, begging God that she might become pregnant. Once she was beseeching the Lord so passionately and with so many tears that the prophet Eli assumed she was intoxicated. He upbraided her: "How long will you make a drunken spectacle of yourself? Put away your wine." It would be hard to imagine a more miserable scenario for Hannah: not only is she agonizing over her unfortunate situation, but she is publicly humiliated by the leading religious authority in the temple. Displaying extraordinary courage, she stands her ground: "No, my lord, I am a woman deeply troubled; I have drunk neither wine nor strong drink, but I have been pouring out my soul before the Lord." She had been praying this prayer: "O Lord of hosts, if only you will look on the misery of your servant, and remember me, and not forget your servant, but will give to your servant a male child, then I will set him before you as a nazirite until the day of his death." (A nazirite was the ancient Israelite version of a monk, someone utterly dedicated to God and God's service.)

Yahweh heard her prayer, and in due time Hannah conceived and bore a son, whom she named Samuel, meaning "desired of the Lord." And when Samuel was weaned, his mother, in fulfillment of her vow, brought him to the temple and gave him to Eli to be raised as a man of God. We know, of course, that Samuel grew to be one of the most pivotal and powerful figures in the history of Israel, playing a key role in the careers of Saul and David and setting the tone for so many of the prophets who would follow him.

Samuel was the son that his mother desired with all her heart, the child for whom she begged year after year. When she held him for the first time in her arms, she must have felt, with special fierceness, that almost mystical connection that mothers have with their children. And yet, despite this bond, she let him go. Despite the wrenching emotions she must have experienced, she allowed him to find his mission according to the will and purpose of God.

On the Feast of the Holy Family, the Church invites us to read the Hannah story in tandem with the account of Mary and Joseph finding the child Jesus in the temple, and the juxtaposition is enlightening. Looking desperately for their lost son over the course of three days, enduring sleepless nights, envisioning over and again the worst possible scenarios, Mary and Joseph must have experienced the darkest of emotions. Thus, when they finally track him down in the temple precincts, debating with the elders, they are understandably exasperated. Mary chastises him: "Child, why have you treated us like this? Look, your father and I have been searching for you in great anxiety." But Jesus appears oblivious to their frantic emotions and replies with devastating brevity: "Why were you searching for me? Did you not know that I must be in my Father's house?" (Luke 2:48–49).

Once more, despite the intense feelings of his mother, a child finds his place in the temple. In both narratives, what is being dramatically called into question is the primacy of emotion and personal feeling in determining a child's life. What matters above all, the Bible teaches over and again, is to find one's mission—and nothing, not even the strongest familial bonds, ought to obstruct that task. Sentiment, however legitimate and understandable, devolves into self-regarding sentimentality when it takes primacy over the purposes of God.

With these counterintuitive stories of Mary and Hannah in mind, let us consider a few of Jesus' own choice comments about families. When a prospective disciple asks for leave to bury his father—an act of piety as highly prized in first-century Jewish culture as it is in ours—Jesus replies with a bluntness that we could only characterize as deeply insensitive: "Follow me, and let the dead bury their own dead" (Matt. 8:22). When a woman cries out enthusiastically, "Blessed is the womb that bore you and the breasts that nursed you," Jesus fires back, "Blessed rather are those who hear the word of God and obey it" (Luke 11:27–28). On still another occasion, when his disciples say, "Your mother and your brothers and sisters are outside, asking for you," Jesus replies, "Who are my mother and my brothers? . . . Whoever does the will of God is my brother and sister and mother" (Mark 3:32–33, 35). And most devastatingly: "Do not think that I have come to bring peace to the earth; I have not come to bring peace, but a sword. For I have come to set a man against his father, and a daughter against her mother" (Matt. 10:34–35). What could these blistering and provocative comments possibly mean? In line with the biblical principle we have been exposing, Jesus insists upon the proper prioritization of spiritual values. To listen to the Word of God, to follow after the Messiah, to do the will of the Lord are the supreme goods, and they must not be compromised by, or rendered secondary to, any other good. In order to test his disciples, therefore, Jesus purposely contrasts the Gospel call to those most emotionally precious and ethically compelling values that obtain within families. Even these—especially these—must give way before the demands of God. Nowhere is this principle more succinctly summarized than in this saying of the Lord: "Whoever loves father or mother more than me is not worthy of me; and whoever loves son or daughter more than me is not worthy of me" (Matt. 10:37).

Given this biblical reading, it is easy enough to see what typically goes wrong with families. A father might be striving to realize his frustrated athletic or professional dreams through his son, thereby reducing his child to a means for the attainment of a self-centered end. A mother might be driving a daughter to perfection in all things, failing all the while to see that her child is collapsing under the pressure. In order to maintain a superficial peace, or simply because they're too lazy or bored to care, parents don't address the dysfunctional behavior of their children. Or a son can use his parents as a source of financial or emotional security, caring nothing for their well-being. In all of these cases, something other than the flourishing of the other is paramount; something other than divine mission—pleasure, pride, success, the working out of psychological frustration—is placed at the center of familial concern. This is precisely the manner in which families become an obstacle to God's intentions and have to be placed rather radically in question.

John Paul II said often that the family is meant to be an *ecclesiola*—a little church. This means that the family is the forum in which the worship of God is the supreme value and the discernment of mission is the supreme task. Parents should realize that their first responsibility is to shape their children not so much for worldly accomplishment but for God's work. And they should, therefore, cultivate the emotional detachment necessary to these ends—and demonstrate the quality so clearly on display in both Hannah and Mary: the willingness to let their children remain in the temple.

Reflection
Pope St. Paul VI
Address

Nazareth is a kind of school where we may begin to discover what Christ's life was like and even to understand his Gospel. Here we can observe and ponder the simple appeal of the way God's Son came to be known, profound yet full of hidden meaning. And gradually we may even learn to imitate him.

Here we can learn to realize who Christ really is. And here we can sense and take account of the conditions and circumstances that surrounded and affected his life on earth: the places, the tenor of the times, the culture, the language, religious customs, in brief everything which Jesus used to make himself known to the world. Here everything speaks to us, everything has meaning. Here we can learn the importance of spiritual discipline for all who wish to follow Christ and to live by the teachings of his Gospel.

How I would like to return to my childhood and attend the simple yet profound school that is Nazareth! How wonderful to be close to Mary, learning again the lesson of the true meaning of life, learning again God's truths. But here we are only on pilgrimage. Time presses and I must set aside my desire to stay and carry on my education in the Gospel, for that education is never finished. But I cannot leave without recalling, briefly and in passing, some thoughts I take with me from Nazareth.

First, we learn from its silence. If only we could once again appreciate its great value. We need this wonderful state of mind, beset as we are by the cacophony of strident protests and conflicting claims so characteristic of these turbulent times. The silence of Nazareth should teach us how to meditate in peace and quiet, to reflect on the deeply spiritual, and to be open to the voice of God's inner wisdom and the counsel of his true teachers. Nazareth can teach us the value of study and preparation, of meditation, of a well-ordered personal spiritual life, and of silent prayer that is known only to God.

Second, we learn about family life. May Nazareth serve as a model of what the family should be. May it show us the family's holy and enduring character and exemplify its basic function in society: a community of love and sharing, beautiful for the problems it poses and the rewards it brings; in sum, the perfect setting for rearing children—and for this there is no substitute.

Finally, in Nazareth, the home of a craftsman's son, we learn about work and the discipline it entails. I would especially like to recognize its value—demanding yet redeeming—and to give it proper respect. I would remind everyone that work has its own dignity. On the other hand, it is not an end in itself. Its value and free character, however, derive not only from its place in the economic system, as they say, but rather from the purpose it serves.

In closing, may I express my deep regard for people everywhere who work for a living. To them I would point out their great model, Christ their brother, our Lord and God, who is their prophet in every cause that promotes their well being.

Poem

Paul Claudel
"Saint Joseph"

When the tools are put in their places and the day's work
    is done,

When between Carmel and the Jordan, Israel falls asleep
    in the wheatfields and the night,

As when he was once a young boy and it began to get too
    dark for reading,

Joseph enters with a deep sight into conversation with God.

He preferred Wisdom and she had been brought to him for
    marriage.

He is as silent as the earth when the dew rises,

He feels the fullness of night, and he is at ease with joy and
    with truth.

Mary is in his possession and he surrounds her on all sides.

It is not in a single day he learned how not to be alone
    anymore.

A woman won over each part of his heart which is now
    prudent and fatherly.

Again he is in Paradise with Eve!

The face which all men need turns with love and submission
    toward Joseph.

It is no longer the same prayer and no longer the ancient
    waiting since he has felt

Like an arm suddenly without hate the pressure of his profound and innocent being.

It is no longer bare Faith in the night, it is love explaining and working.

Joseph is with Mary and Mary is with the Father.

And for us, too, so that God at last may be allowed, whose works surpass our reason,

So that this light may not be extinguished by our lamp and His word by the noise we make,

So that man cease, and Your kingdom come and Your Will be done,

So that we may find again the beginning with boundless delight,

So that the sea may quiet down and Mary begin,

She who has the better part and who consummates the struggle of ancient Israel,

Inner Patriarch, Joseph, obtain silence for us!

Hymn

O Lux Beata Caelitum

Latin

O Lux beata caelitum
Et summa spes mortalium,
Iesu, o cui domestica
Arrisit orto caritas:

Maria, dives gratia
O sola quae casto potes
Fovere Iesum pectore,
Cum lacte donans oscula:

Tuque ex vetustis patribus
Delecte custos Virginis,
Dulci patris quem nomine
Divina Proles invocat:

De stirpe Iesse nobili
Nati in salutem gentium,
Audite nos, qui supplices
Vestras ad aras sistimus.

English

O highest Hope of mortals,
Blest Light of saints above,
O Jesus, on whose boyhood
Home smiled with kindly love;

And thou whose bosom nursed him,
O Mary, highly graced,
Whose breast gave milk to Jesus,
Whose arms thy God embraced;

And thou of all men chosen
To guard the Virgin's fame,
To whom God's Son refused not
A Father's gracious name;

Born for the nations' healing,
Of Jesse's lineage high,
Behold the suppliants kneeling,
O hear the sinners' cry!

Dum sol redux ad vesperum
Rebus nitorem detrahit,
Nos hic manentes intimo
Ex corde vota fundimus.

Qua vestra sedes floruit
Virtutis omnis gratia,
Hanc detur in domesticis
Referre posse moribus.

Iesu, tuis obediens
Qui factus es parentibus,
Cum Patre summo ac Spiritu
Semper tibi sit gloria.

The sun returned to evening,
Dusks all the twilight air:
We, lingering here before you,
Pour out our heartfelt prayer.

Your home was as a garden
Made glad with fairest flowers;
May life thus blossom sweetly
In every home of ours.

All praise to thee, O Jesus,
Who parents dost obey;
Praise to the sovereign Father
And Paraclete for aye.

Reflection

St. Teresa of Avila

The Life of St. Teresa, Written by Herself

Would that I could persuade all men to be devout to this glorious saint; for I know by long experience what blessings he can obtain for us from God. I have never known anyone who was really devout to him, and who honored him by particular services, who did not visibly grow more and more in virtue; for he helps in a special way those souls who commend themselves to him. It is now some years since I have always on his feast asked him for something, and I always have it. If the petition be in any way amiss, he directs it aright for my greater good.

If I were a person who had authority to write, it would be a pleasure to me to be diffusive in speaking most minutely of the graces which this glorious saint has obtained for me and for others. . . . But I ask, for the love of God, that he who does not believe me will make the trial for himself—when he will see by experience the great good that results from commending oneself to this glorious patriarch, and being devout to him. Those who give themselves to prayer should in a special manner have always a devotion to St. Joseph; for I know not how any man can think of the Queen of the angels, during the time that she suffered so much with the Infant Jesus, without giving thanks to St. Joseph for the services he rendered them then. He who cannot find anyone to teach him how to pray, let him take this glorious saint for his master, and he will not wander out of the way.

Prayer
Pope Francis
Amoris Laetitia

Jesus, Mary, and Joseph,
in you we contemplate
the splendor of true love;
to you we turn with trust.
Holy Family of Nazareth,
grant that our families too
may be places of communion and prayer,
authentic schools of the Gospel,
and small domestic churches.

Holy Family of Nazareth,
may families never again experience
violence, rejection, and division;
may all who have been hurt or scandalized
find ready comfort and healing.

Holy Family of Nazareth,
make us once more mindful

of the sacredness and inviolability of the family,
and its beauty in God's plan.

Jesus, Mary, and Joseph,
Graciously hear our prayer.
Amen.

Poem

G.K. Chesterton
"A Little Litany"

When God turned back eternity and was young,
    Ancient of Days, grown little for your mirth
(As under the low arch the land is bright)
    Peered through you, gate of heaven—and saw the earth.

Or shutting out his shining skies awhile
    Built you about him for a house of gold
To see in pictured walls his storied world
    Return upon him as a tale is told.

Or found his mirror there; the only glass
    That would not break with that unbearable light
Till in a corner of the high dark house
    God looked on God, as ghosts meet in the night.

Star of his morning; that unfallen star
    In the strange starry overturn of space
When earth and sky changed places for an hour
    And heaven looked upwards in a human face.

Or young on your strong knees and lifted up
    Wisdom cried out, whose voice is in the street,
And more than twilight of twiformed cherubim
    Made of his throne indeed a mercy-seat.

Or risen from play at your pale raiment's hem
    God, grown adventurous from all time's repose,
Of your tall body climbed the ivory tower
    And kissed upon your mouth the mystic rose.

"Christ chose to be born and grow up in the bosom of the holy family of Joseph and Mary. The Church is nothing other than 'the family of God.'"

—*CATECHISM OF THE CATHOLIC CHURCH*

Conclusion

Friends, thank you for joining us on this journey. Now that Advent and Christmas are over, you might be wondering, what's next? How do I maintain the spiritual momentum? I'd like to suggest a few practical tips.

First, be sure to visit our website, WordOnFire.org, on a regular basis. There you'll find lots of helpful resources, including new articles, videos, blog posts, podcasts, and homilies, all designed to help strengthen your faith and evangelize the culture. The best part is that all of it is free!

In addition to those free resources, I invite you to join the Word on Fire Institute. This is an online hub of deep spiritual and intellectual formation, where you'll journey through courses taught by me and other Fellows. Our goal is to build an army of evangelists, people who have been transformed by Christ and want to bring his light to the world. Learn more and sign up at https://wordonfire.institute.

Finally, the best way to carry on your progress is to commit to at least one new spiritual practice. For instance, you might read through one of the Gospels, one chapter per day; or start praying part of the Liturgy of the Hours; or spend some time with the Blessed Sacrament once a week; or decide to attend one extra Mass each week; or pray one

Rosary each day. All of these are simple, straightforward ways to deepen your spiritual life.

Again, thank you from all of us at Word on Fire, and God bless you!

Peace,

Bishop Robert Barron

Additional Prayers

O Antiphons

The Roman Church has been singing the "O" Antiphons since at least the eighth century. They are the antiphons that accompany the *Magnificat* canticle of Evening Prayer from December 17–23. They are a magnificent theology that uses ancient biblical imagery drawn from the messianic hopes of the Old Testament to proclaim the coming Christ as the fulfillment not only of Old Testament hopes, but present ones as well. Their repeated use of the imperative "Come!" embodies the longing of all for the Divine Messiah.

December 17: *O Sapientia*

Latin

O Sapientia, quae ex ore Altissimi prodiisti, attingens a fine usque ad finem, fortiter suaviterque disponens omnia: veni ad docendum nos viam prudentiae.

English

O Wisdom, O holy Word of God, you govern all creation with your strong and tender care. Come and show your people the way to salvation.

December 18: *O Adonai*

Latin

O Adonai, et Dux domus Israel, qui Moysi in igne flammae rubi apparuisti, et ei in Sina legem dedisti: veni ad redimendum nos in brachio extento.

English

O sacred Lord of ancient Israel, who showed yourself to Moses in the burning bush, who gave him the holy law on Sinai mountain: come, stretch out your mighty hand to set us free.

December 19: *O Radix Iesse*

Latin

O radix Iesse, qui stas in signum populorum, super quem continebunt reges os suum, quem Gentes deprecabuntur: veni ad liberandum nos, iam noli tardare.

English

O Flower of Jesse's stem, you have been raised up as a sign for all peoples; kings stand silent in your presence; the nations bow down to worship before you. Come, let nothing keep you from coming to our aid.

December 20: *O Clavis David*

Latin

O Clavis David, et sceptrum domus Israel; qui aperis, et nemo claudit; claudis, et nemo aperit: veni, et educ vinctum de domo carceris, sedentem in tenebris et umbra mortis.

English

O Key of David, O royal Power of Israel controlling at your will the gate of heaven: come, break down the prison walls of death for those who dwell in darkness and the shadow of death; and lead your captive people into freedom.

December 21: *O Oriens*

Latin

O Oriens, splendor lucis aeternae, et sol iustitiae: veni, et illumina sedentes in tenebris, et umbra mortis.

English

O Radiant Dawn, splendor of the eternal light, sun of justice: come, shine on those who dwell in darkness and the shadow of death.

December 22: *O Rex Gentium*

Latin

O Rex Gentium, et desideratus earum, lapisque angularis, qui facis utraque unum: veni, et salva hominem, quem de limo formasti.

English

O King of all nations, the only joy of every human heart; O Keystone of the mighty arch of man, come and save the creature you fashioned from the dust.

December 23: *O Emmanuel*

Latin

O Emmanuel, Rex et legifer noster, exspectatio Gentium, et Salvator earum: veni ad salvandum nos, Domine, Deus noster.

English

O Emmanuel, king and lawgiver, desire of the nations, Savior of all people, come and set us free, Lord our God.

The Angelus

℣. The Angel of the Lord declared unto Mary,
℟. And she conceived by the Holy Spirit.

Hail Mary, full of grace, the Lord is with thee;
blessed art thou among women,
and blessed is the fruit of thy womb, Jesus.
Holy Mary, Mother of God,
pray for us sinners
now and at the hour of our death.
Amen.

℣. Behold the handmaid of the Lord,
℟. Be it done unto me according to thy Word.

Hail Mary . . .

℣. And the Word was made flesh,
℟. And dwelt among us.

Hail Mary . . .

℣. Pray for us, O holy Mother of God,
℟. That we may be made worthy of the promises of Christ.

Let us pray. Pour forth, we beseech thee, O Lord, thy grace into our hearts: that we, to whom the Incarnation of Christ thy Son was made known by the message of an angel, may by his Passion and Cross be brought to the glory of his Resurrection. Through the same Christ our Lord.

Amen.

The Memorare

Remember, O most gracious Virgin Mary, that never was it known that anyone who fled to thy protection, implored thy help, or sought thy intercession, was left unaided.

Inspired by this confidence, I fly unto thee, O Virgin of virgins, my Mother.

To thee do I come, before thee I stand, sinful and sorrowful.

O Mother of the Word Incarnate, despise not my petitions, but in thy mercy hear and answer me.

Amen.

Notes

Minor adjustments have occasionally been made on excerpted material for consistency and readability.

The First Week of Advent: The Messiah

Reading: Robert Barron, "Doing Some Real Advent Spiritual Work," Word on Fire, December 1, 2020, https://www.wordonfire.org/articles/barron/doing-some-real-advent-spiritual-work/.

Reflection: Fulton J. Sheen, *Life of Christ* (Park Ridge, IL: Word on Fire Classics, 2018), 2–3.

Poem: Thomas Merton, "Advent," in *The Collected Poems of Thomas Merton* (New York: New Directions, 1980), 88.

Hymn: *Liturgy of the Hours*, vol. 1, *Advent Season / Christmas Season* (New York: Catholic Book Publishing Co., 1975), 129–131.

Reflection: John Paul II, "Homily of His Holiness John Paul II during the Mass for University Students and Professors," December 12, 1996, vatican.va.

Prayer: John Henry Newman, *Meditations and Devotions* (New York: Longmans & Green, 1893), 401–402.

Poem: G.K. Chesterton, "A Child of the Snows," in *Poems* (New York: John Lane Company, 1916), 83.

Quote: Edith Stein, *The Collected Works of Edith Stein*, vol. 4, *The Hidden Life: Essays, Meditations, Spiritual Texts*, ed. L. Gelber and Michael Linssen, trans. Waltraut Stein (Washington, DC: ICS, 2014), 109.

The Second Week of Advent: The Annunciation

Reading: Robert Barron, *Light from Light: A Theological Reflection on the Nicene Creed* (Park Ridge, IL: Word on Fire Academic, 2021), 44–45.

Reflection: Gregory Thaumaturgus, "Four Homilies," trans. S.D.F. Salmond, in Ante-Nicene Fathers, vol. 6, ed. Alexander Roberts, James Donaldson, and A. Cleveland Coxe (Buffalo, NY: Christian Literature, 1886), newadvent.org.

Poem: Dante, *Paradise*, Canto 33, trans. Anthony Esolen (New York: Modern Library, 2007), 351.

Hymn: *Liturgy of the Hours*, vol. 1, 1189.

Reflection: *Liturgy of the Hours*, vol. 1, December 20, Office of Readings, 345–346.

Prayer: Mother Teresa, *Love: A Fruit Always in Season: Daily Meditations by Mother Teresa*, ed. Dorothy S. Hunt (San Francisco: Ignatius, 1987), 164.

Poem: G.K. Chesterton, "Regina Angelorum," in *The Queen of Seven Swords* (London: Sheed & Ward, 1926), 18–19.

Quote: Irenaeus, *Against Heresies* 3.22.4, trans. Alexander Roberts and William Rambaut, in Ante-Nicene Fathers, vol. 1, ed. Alexander Roberts, James Donaldson, and A. Cleveland Coxe (Buffalo, NY: Christian Literature, 1885), newadvent.org.

The Third Week of Advent: The Incarnation

Reading: Robert Barron, *Catholicism: A Journey to the Heart of the Faith* (New York: Image Books, 2011), 1–4.

Reflection: Athanasius, *On the Incarnation of the Word* 54, trans. Archibald Robertson, in Nicene and Post-Nicene Fathers, Second Series, vol. 4, ed. Philip Schaff and Henry Wace (Buffalo, NY: Christian Literature, 1892), newadvent.org.

Poem: John of the Cross, "Ballad on the Gospel" VII, in Gerald Brenan, *St. John of the Cross: His Life and Poetry*, trans. Lynda Nicholson (Cambridge: Cambridge University Press, 1973), 201, 203.

Hymn: *Liturgy of the Hours*, vol. 1, 127–129.

Reflection: Bonaventure, *The Tree of Life*, in *Bonaventure: The Soul's Journey into God; The Tree of Life; The Life of St. Francis*, trans. Ewert Cousins (Mahwah, NJ: Paulist), 126–128.

Prayer: Catherine of Siena, *Catherine of Siena: The Dialogue*, trans. Suzanne Noffke (Mahwah, NJ: Paulist, 1980), 49–50.

Poem: G.K. Chesterton, "Gloria in Profundis," in *Collected Works*, vol. 10, *Collected Poetry: Part I* (San Francisco: Ignatius, 1994), 137–138.

Quote: Flannery O'Connor, *The Habit of Being: Letters of Flannery O'Connor* (New York: Farrar, Straus & Giroux, 1979), 360.

The Fourth Week of Advent: The Journey to Bethlehem

Reading: Robert Barron, *Light from Light*, 72–74.

Reflection: Joseph Ratzinger, *Jesus of Nazareth: The Infancy Narratives*, trans. Philip Whitmore (New York: Image Books, 2012), 58–59, 64.

Poem: Gerard Manley Hopkins, "Moonless Darkness," in *Collected Works*, vol. 3, *Diaries, Journals, & Notebooks* (Oxford: Oxford University Press, 2015), 341.

Hymn: Richard L. Crocker, *An Introduction to Gregorian Chant* (New Haven, CT: Yale University Press, 2000), 211.

Reflection: Thomas Aquinas, *Summa theologiae* 3.35.7, trans. Fathers of the English Dominican Province (London: Burns, Oates, and Washbourne, 1920), newadvent.org.

Prayer: Francis, *Patris Corde*, apostolic letter, December 8, 2020, vatican.va.

Poem: G.K. Chesterton, "The House of Christmas," in *Collected Works*, 10:139–140.

Quote: Origen, *Homilies on Leviticus 1–16*, trans. Gary Wayne Barkley (Washington, DC: The Catholic University of America Press, 1990), 160.

Christmas Day: The Nativity

Reading: Robert Barron, *Vibrant Paradoxes: The Both/And of Catholicism* (Skokie, IL: Word on Fire, 2017), 132–135.

Reflection: G.K. Chesterton, *The Everlasting Man* (San Francisco: Ignatius, 1993), 169–172.

Poem: Thérèse of Lisieux, "The Little Divine Beggar of Christmas," in *Poems of St. Teresa, Carmelite of Lisieux* (Boston: Angel Guardian, 1907), 127–128, 131, https://ccel.org/ccel/therese/poems/poems.i.html.

Hymn: *The Hymns of the Breviary and Missal*, ed. Matthew Britt (New York: Benziger Brothers, 1952), 86–87.

Reflection: *Liturgy of the Hours*, vol. 1, December 24, Office of Readings, 379–381.

Prayer: John XXIII, *Journal of a Soul: The Autobiography of Pope John XXIII*, trans. Dorothy White (New York: Geoffrey Chapman, 2000), 393.

Poem: G.K. Chesterton, "A Xmas Carol," in *Collected Works*, 10:126.

Quote: Hebrews 1:1–2.

The Christmas Season: The Holy Family

Reading: Robert Barron, *Proclaiming the Power of Christ: Classic Sermons* (Word on Fire Institute, 2021), 133–136.

Reflection: *Liturgy of the Hours*, vol. 1, Feast of the Holy Family, Office of Readings, 426–428.

Poem: Paul Claudel, "Saint Joseph," in *Poetry* 87, no. 3 (December 1955): 140–141.

Hymn: *Hymns of the Breviary and Missal*, 100–101.

Reflection: Teresa of Avila, *The Life of S. Teresa of Jesus of the Order of our Lady of Carmel, Written by Herself*, trans. David Lewis (London: Burns, Oates & Co., 1870), 35.

Prayer: Francis, *Amoris Laetitia*, encyclical letter, March 19, 2016, vatican.va.

Poem: Chesterton, "A Little Litany," in *Queen of Seven Swords*, 14.

Quote: *Catechism of the Catholic Church* 1655.

Additional Prayers

O Antiphons: *Liturgy of the Hours*, vol. 1, December 17, Evening Prayer, Canticle of Mary Antiphon, 325, 333, 342, 350, 358, 367.

The Angelus: "Angelus," United States Conference of Catholic Bishops website, https://www.usccb.org/prayers/angelus.

The Memorare: "Memorare," United States Conference of Catholic Bishops website, https://www.usccb.org/prayers/memorare.